On M

G000155693

Steven Matthews is a poet and critic born and brought up in Colchester, Essex. He has been a regular reviewer of poetry for *London Magazine*, *Poetry Review*, and the *TLS*, as well as Poetry Editor for *Dublin Quarterly Magazine*. Waterloo Press published his first collection, *Skying*, in 2012.

Also by Two Rivers Poets:

David Attwooll, *The Sound Ladder* (2015)

Kate Behrens, *The Beholder* (2012)

Kate Behrens, *Man with Bombe Alaska* (2016)

Adrian Blamires, *The Effect of Coastal Processes* (2005)

Adrian Blamires, *The Pang Valley* (2010)

Adrian Blamires & Peter Robinson (eds.), *The Arts of Peace* (2014)

Joseph Butler, *Hearthstone* (2006)

David Cooke, *A Murmuration* (2015)

Terry Cree, *Fruit* (2014)

Jane Draycott and Lesley Saunders, *Christina the Astonishing* (1998)

Jane Draycott, *Tideway* (2002)

Claire Dyer, *Eleven Rooms* (2013)

Claire Dyer, *Interference Effects* (2016)

John Froy, *Eggshell: A Decorator's Notes* (2007)

A. F. Harrold, *Logic and the Heart* (2004)

A. F. Harrold, *Flood* (2009)

A. F. Harrold, *The Point of Inconvenience* (2013)

Ian House, *Cutting the Quick* (2005)

Ian House, *Nothing's Lost* (2014)

Gill Learner, *The Agister's Experiment* (2011)

Gill Learner, *Chill Factor* (2016)

Becci Louise, *Octopus Medicine* (2017)

Mairi MacInnes, *Amazing Memories of Childhood, etc.* (2016)

Henri Michaux, *Storms under the Skin* translated by Jane Draycott (2017)

Tom Phillips, *Recreation Ground* (2012)

John Pilling and Peter Robinson (eds.), *The Rilke of Ruth Speirs:*
   New Poems, Duino Elegies, Sonnets to Orpheus & Others (2015)

Peter Robinson, *English Nettles and Other Poems* (2010)

Peter Robinson (ed.), *Reading Poetry: An Anthology* (2011)

Peter Robinson (ed.), *A Mutual Friend: Poems for Charles Dickens* (2012)

Peter Robinson, *Foreigners, Drunks and Babies: Eleven Stories* (2013)

Robert Seatter, *The Book of Snow* (2016)

Lesley Saunders, *Her Leafy Eye* (2009)

Lesley Saunders, *Cloud Camera* (2012)

Susan Utting, *Houses Without Walls* (2006)

Susan Utting, *Fair's Fair* (2012)

Susan Utting, *Half the Human Race* (2017)

Jean Watkins, *Scrimshaw* (2013)

On Magnetism

Steven Matthews

TWO
RIVERS
PRESS

First published in the UK in 2017 by Two Rivers Press
7 Denmark Road, Reading RG1 5PA.
www.tworiverspress.com

ISBN 978-1-909747-32-6

1 2 3 4 5 6 7 8 9

Two Rivers Press is represented in the UK by Inpress Ltd
and distributed by NBNi.

Cover design by Nadja Guggi based on an illustration drawn from
De Magnete by William Gilbert
Text design by Nadja Guggi and typeset in Janson and Parisine

Printed and bound in Great Britain by Imprint Digital, Exeter

That
this fine mechanism –
amygdalae, cerebellum,
the parietal or occipital lobe –
each to each speaking
in series
            its story

might tilt
            its switches

and disorder itself,
its knownness not now known,
its histories de-written

Acknowledgements

Earlier versions of some of these poems have appeared in a number of publications, journals and anthologies, including *Stand, Poetry and Audience*, *Origami Warriors*, *From the City to the Saltings: Poems from Essex*, *To This Quiet Spot*, *The Arts of Peace*, *Guests of Time* (Valley Press), and *Ceaseless Music* (Bloomsbury).

The central sonnet sequence, 'William Gilbert: *On Magnetism*', was read as part of the 'Poets on the Past' series at the London Shakespeare Seminar in November 2013. 'Looking at Late Rembrandts (after leaving Dad at the Nursing Home)' was an Oxford Brookes 'Weekly Poem'.

I am deeply grateful, for their comments on drafts of the poems, to Helen Farish and Elleke Boehmer and Peter Robinson. This book is dedicated to Elleke with love.

Contents

Erato

She comes to this quiet spot each afternoon
in summer, sets her stool on the stamped soil path,
and checks the tuning of her guitar.

Passers-by soon group in anticipation,
bored parents pause pushchairs, and rest on them.
A few chords, but still the song does not begin.

She gazes a long time toward the shimmer
in sunlight at the end of the path, to where
the words might come from, words

for the lovelornness that could then well
from her, drawing the tune and the beauty
that re-cast the demarcations of the day.

In Dad's Boots

He gave me them at the start of the last
summer, sagged on his walker, his shaking hands
handing on these means to his brief freedoms
in the mountains, on his few trips abroad.

Now, resurrected from the back of the shed,
they walk me hobblingly through a day
of streaming roads and fields, into the silence
of a crouched church, whose timbered roof

is the roof of a barn, its stilled force
holding and resisting the distempered
landscape, mud and slipperiness, sunfreaks
across valleys buttercupping meadows.

A Rare One With Flowers

(i.m. Dorothy Scott neé Airey)

I.

Your life spanned from the child-crammed terrace
to nursing your mother, to house-maiding
and late marriage, tending your ill husband.

Across the years of silent devotion
and arrangements, your concern was to make
sure that all ran like clockwork for others.

The slow tick-tock of afternoons with you,
the sudden explosion of chimes each hour
from the grandmother clock in the back room;

your silence was only broken near the end,
to tell of wondrous sightings of Zeppelins
on your runs to school through blossoming fields.

II.

Your two step-children and niece linger long,
circling and shuffling before the few wreaths,
Essex sea-winds cutting across the tarmac.

All that alleviates the bland account
of your life by the priest, is the delight
you took in arranging your garden's flowers: so,

beside the poor tributes propped on the path,
I lay down chrysanths, stocks, delphiniums,
gladioli, hollyhocks, dahlias,

daffodils, roses, nasturtiums, lilies,
pansies, sweet peas, carnations, wall flowers,
geraniums, peonies, irises,

fox gloves, bluebells, violets, hyacinths,
dahlias, amaryllis, stocks, lilies –
all the flowers I know, for you to gather elsewhere.

3

Night Journey

As a fast young runner,
you came to love the breath-
lessness of being sped
up hills in buses' wakes,

sprinting up close behind
then accelerating
into the slope, jumping
on their step at the top.

As I drove on the night
of your death, to the place
I found your body was
already removed from,

I stayed in the slipstream
of an articulat-
ed lorry, my small car
held in its steadfast wake.

The Aeolian Harp at Dove Cottage

Extreme quietness entered the headphones,
time paused between breaths. Then, a quavering breeze
sent its recorded sigh through the casement,
like a player warming an instrument.
Single strings first raised hesitant music
as the machine's tape wakened into life;
wavering notes, as when friends tentatively
dance on the threshold of a declared love.

The desultory breeze grew bolder,
the strings vibrated from chords through discords
to a happy return of harmony,
a surprising interfusion of sweet with harsh,
as the wind lessened its threatening force
to strange-sung notes of peacefulness.

Transported myself by this utterance,
I called you over to hear it sound,
and watched your tired face open in rapt joy.
After our day of chill slanting showers,
climbing the steep hillside to the tarn
with live writhing waters rushing all round,
all at last settled into pensive quiet,
into quickening, shared wonder.

Laugharne

Rain rifled through the shivering oak leaves
we sheltered under, on the path
from the blue boathouse, where curled postcards
showed the faded shapes of loved poets' heads
wreathed in cobweb strings and blackened shorelight.

Then, suddenly, the sun's emerged glare set
the path's flint-stones sparking, and we returned
to be blinded by the window's rare
illumination; the gleam from his plain
worktable, the poets' faces shining out.

A Late Work

(Van Gogh)

Wheatfields: the broad landscape of yellow
or green or mottled dotted flowers
divided by broad strokes of red
or black, the brush-hairs crushed
so hard into canvas they've shed strands
in the embossed paint;

prone beneath thunder-head skies,
clouds smeary with black,
the rooks' crude-vee'd wings
fugitives in front
of the already-gathered and worked
blue blank future.

Sounding the Canal

Five harsh days of hard frosts,
the canal path a glistening ribbon
of solid mud, the canal's crystalline
surface parading
the canal-bed's detritus –
logs, branches, a bike frame,
rocks of clumped earth,
a tracery of skeletal leaves
bolted into the solid substance.

Only when you began prising
small pebbles out of the path from
their thumb-print mud pebble-beds
and skimming them swiftly across
the frosted canal surface, was life
to be re-heard:
dull-zingings, light dashes of sound
sounded deep through the canal's base
echoing beneath and beyond
the canal bridge,
                    disturbing
the out-of-their depth, ice-bewildered
geese to clatter into air.

Kinetophonographia

Attendant silence
Around the flat-watered pond
The mannered ease of
Late Victorian Sundays,
The fine chink of teaspoon
On bone-china paused
At tables flowering in the Park.

The carefully draped
Marble figures, the nymphs
And fauns, the soldiers
And statesmen, stand
Alert on their plinths,
Poised ready to perform.

Mahogany loudspeakers are strapped
Hard against the statues' bases.
At the simultaneous release
Of the apparatus's sounds,
Small tremors set the stone
Vibrating, projecting noise

Out across quelled air,
Peoples' breath arrested
By the ground bass's seismic
Eruption, marble animate
With arias scored from beyond.

Winter Branches

Upset at being made
        to think of them
as crooked,
silhouetted skeletons' fingers
pleading up
        into a blind sky

I am waiting
for the knuckles of the buds
to split, for
their leaves, then red blossom,
        to flare out

Migrations

(Isabel Lambert)

Two swallows perch on
the bedroom windowsill
at Sudbury Cottage,

fragile before
the coming winter storms.
Hands ring them,

cup, then release
them into some otherwhere,
their only haven

a port-of-call
island, its cliffs a thick line
where blue of sea is

jointed with blue of sky.
And, upon their return,
the stubble is not yet

being burnt in black
billows of clogging smoke
behind the Cottage,

and pesticides do not yet
run from the land
into the rivers,

plunging gulls
dead amongst the hemlock.
Rape seed burgeons,

along with cow parsley,
cranesbill, wild poppies.
The swallows waltz,

suspended in the cerulean,
as though angels
or hawks,

their skeletons etched
by brush-handle-point
within their frail forms.

Airs

New words to some madrigals by John Wilbye

I.

My school recorder crunched under my dumb foot,
Its plastic mouthpiece shattered at the base;
But, in our poverty, we could have no thought
Of buying a new, for me to save face.
So Dad made the recorder a metal joint.
So I sound sharp or flat, never the true note.

II.

When will the cancer strike, burst aorta
Slowly drown me in my own blood, Parkinson's
Calcify my brain until I'm stunned a-
Way from what I am, gaping at someone's
Face who claims she's what I love? Kind sickness,
That would cure me quickly of life's illness.

III.

When you died, it was impossible
To find the words to speak about
Those final six months, the hospital,
Then, in the nursing home, the bout
Of fits and half-coma, before your death
Took from our voices all their sounding breath.

My mind calls to you each day,
Sees you still in the life with us
From which yet you are gone astray;
But when I try to hear your voice
In my thoughts or daydreams, it is as though you
Can only moan in pain, before silence takes you.

Into the Dark

The more I pull you in to me,
the more quickly you move away,

dark energy accelerating you the more
rapidly from my grappling arms,

you becoming lost to my senses of you,
the ninety-five percent of the world

that is, yet is not there for us,
blinding you from me,

ever the less
able now to pull you back in close.

Not I

And the dying Virgin Queen became,
in her last days, one in her own retinue;
the stalwart servant who sat in silence
through four days and nights outside her chamber;

from unremovable melancholy

unable to enter and view the false
shadow of herself sprawled into silk pillows,
or to stand, aghast, by her body, aghast,
at the final dreams from its sovereign mind.

The Poker

stood gleaming in the tool stand
on the hearth, clipped beside
the little brush for sweeping the grate,
and the little shovel for stacking the coals.

The armchairs stood huge round the fireplace;
from his, he would lean forward,
release the poker with a sharp click
from that shining steel stand, and reach
to aerate the fading lower coals.

Except Saturday evenings. Saturday evenings,
he would come back late from the whist drive,
slowly remove his coat, and often lay down
his silver winnings on the green tablecloth.

But, if, from the set of his face
as he entered the room, she saw
there were no winnings, she made
to dart upstairs, before the poker

could be brought down across
her spine, across her waist, across her thighs.

Perspective

The clear notes of a song of a blackbird
on a summer's evening, the orange light
purpled beyond the meshed fence, repeated
notes focus receding daytime,
chorusing light through sound,
lamenting perfections lost to time.

And to return to this, this moment again
and again, this captured soundscape,
withdrawing light, the acceding chill,
again across decades, to pitch the self
on that garden bench, to hold the seen and sung

in that set perspective, the scene unmoved,
the birds' notes ever-renewed, opens space
in the mind, vanishing point of memory's
imaginings, the lure of their constant call.

Lear Variations

There is a seagull standing on your sleeve.
That submarine engine needs to be sent parcel post.
Can't you see the giraffe in that tree?
If you have anything else to say
write it down and put it on my desk.
If you hold the thing up like this
(hand-gesture, playing fishing line)
and keep hold of the other end,
then the thing won't ever slip.
"And what did we used to play, Dad,
on quiet Sunday afternoons?"
Table-tennis on the table I made.
Badminton, sometimes bowls.
The sun shone a lot in those days.

II.

When they took me down to the room
the woman sat me on a chair with a gap beside
and when they moved me there was always a gap
to the next person and then the girls
started singing some kind of songs, carols
I remembered in a circle on the floor
but there remained always that gap in the chairs
and by then Grandma and Grandad had
disappeared, gone off somewhere I don't know,
so by the time the girls stopped their singing
there was no one left to take me home
to the other side of the gap where mum
was lying wrapped in blankets round her legs,
her top part, and up to her ears, but then
it snowed when I got outside,
and I got across the white fields home
to the cottage and put the bucket down
into the well and got myself water
to drink, then sat inside in the darkness
to see if anyone would come across

and find me.

Nostalgia

Mind is the stories it tells itself

like those seasick storm-caught sailors
who stepped across the ship's side into green wheat

thrashing in the winds, not one of them glancing back,
but rushing towards loves calling them home

stories it tells as it teaches us not to hear them.

Aftermath

On each weekly visit
to Shrubland Road, the boy fitted
his foot into the dunted place

in the grey concrete of the pavement,
its radiating fissures
lined by clumps of moss.

After rains, its concentrated pool
contained the stalwart row
of terraced houses, slated roofs

blocking unpredictable skies.
This was the street of the elders, great-
grandmother and hair-netted great

aunts in nylon housecoats, determined
to wrestle days into conformity.
But the pavement's dunt remembered for him

the spot where the doodlebug landed
in Forty Four and sat for two days,
its detonator clicking into the silence

between the startled house-fronts,
before its nested threat to all this
could be disarmed,

the space of its aftermath discovered.

Vigil

From out of absent eyes
the herm stares
into the absolute emptiedness
of the triclinium's
high wide cube:

from the red-painted walls
golden comma-strokes
gleam sun on myrtle-
garlands, a brief
flourish of vine.
The sketch in perspective
of theatre-space
encloses sylvae
in heraldic dance
held,
gossamer gowns
bellied by more
light strokes,
in mythological breezes.

Bodiless,
the bronze herm's head
wards time
from the silenced room,
movement, the murals
stern
in their delicacy
within the tons
of lava and pumice.

Those Wonderful Cities

(for Thomas)

When we woke each morning
and went into your room,
you sat, with book in hand,
holding in a wide smile,
not casting your eyes down
towards the beige carpet,
where there stood each morning
fantastical cities
built from your wooden blocks:
yellow towers, tree-flourished
streets, orange bridges, parks,
an all-red tall clock-spire;
cities peopled with blue-
haired people shapes, where cars
with families sped down
empty roads, watched by dogs
and cats from your plastic
animals set; mornings
which made us different worlds.

Colony

We slept in ditches, skirmished
in raiding-parties as they marched on.
Lice-ridden, our hair for once ungroomed.

Our river gods cast us off; so, soon,
they came across the fences of pales
laid by Cunobelinus, above the river's banks.

Close to, they seemed shrunken in leather,
as the cold bit into tanned skins.
We fought naked. But wattle and daub

flared, animals screamed, the corn pits
clogged with ones whose souls flew out
from their heads. Gold torcs and jewels were stamped in mud.

The druids were dragged away,
stories of the ancestors rich
in their minds, stopped in their mouths.

On the feast-day for victory
their emperor entered our walls
throned high on a beast grey as gorse-wood,

its long snout swung nearly to earth.
Our warriors shied before the thunder
of its massive, stubbed feet.

The gods have left the burnt temple –
now only a brick shrine stands there for worship
of the one who lurched above us that dread day.

Bat-Shrieks

One evening during that long, hot, summer
the window was barely inches open,
but yet the small bat, lost in its bearings,
homed straight through into our small, cramped bedroom.
We opened the door on frantic circling,
its high-pitched calls soon outdone by your screams
as the perfect thing, desperate to perch,
fastened its crystal claws into your hair.
Only my desperate grabbings with a towel
had it freed several minutes later
and crammed out through the narrow window slot,
from where it flew off wonkily away.
I hugged you, unsteadily. Our distress,
never to be flung back out, circles pleadingly today.

Inner Town Tudor Courtyard

(for William Bedford)

Locked iron gates, beneath a centuries-worn archway;
a concentration of scents, herbs, flowers,
resonates from the beds beyond their grille.
Summer sun thrummed by bees in the broad space;
the beamed house-fronts, leaded windows, oak doors
stand to the garden's side, blanked by the heat,
shut from the busy-ness of everyday streets.
The pattern of pathways, focal sundial,
are peace conserved against the times, and change.
To be barred out from that yard, but to have peered in
from when I was a wayward child on reins,
centres imagination across all lifetime's revisitings.

William Gilbert: *On Magnetism*

'Hast'ou seen the rose in the steel dust?'
(Ezra Pound, Canto LXXIV)

I.

Place

William Gilbert, town recorder's son,
Born, Fifteen Forty-Four, in Colchester,
Had success, much of his life, in London;
Buried, Holy Trinity, Colchester,

Cause of death, bubonic plague, Sixteen Three.
Court physician to Queen Elizabeth,
He kept the family house called Tymperley,
In his home town, until the day of his death.

He had 'the clearness of Venetian Glass
Without the brittleness thereof', was full
Of perfections. Tymperley's centring force
Drew gatherings of scientists, its courtyard's lull

'Informating' the new philosophy.
Now magnetic Earth spun, empirically.

II.

Legend

No, not after Magnes, who trod the Spring
Earth in his hobnails, following his flock
'Til struck in his tracks, no strength for lifting
Those boots' iron nails clear of the ferrous rock;

Not after Hercules, through its great force
In subduing iron, that dumb hard coldness
Which weighs so heavily amongst Earth's resource,
Yet is lured by invisible caress;

Nor yet after Sideritis, some shard
Showered from the skies, though it glisten like jewels,
That magical iron. Such stories are marred
By contradiction of science's rules:

It's named for magnetite, present all round
The globe, struck by lightning as it hits ground.

III.

Coition

No one can tell what magnetism is;
Fundamental monopoles are unknown.
Yet magnetism proves the Earth *lives*, stars
Move in fixed tracks, and all souls can conjoin.

North and South Poles are like male and female:
Breath from one body touches the other
And they are united, electrical
Effluvia sending peculiar

Radiation which makes two into one,
Just as amber brushed by a cloth attracts
Light. Bodies touching bring us protection
In a magnetic field against all facts

Threatening the universe: flares from the sun,
Or nuclear death stranding Earth stopped, alone.

IV.

Sameness and Difference

Electricity moves from positive
To negative; in all magnetic fields
Circulation of flows moves relative
To the 'verticity' our planet yields.

The speed of electromagnetic waves
Is the same as the speed of light, but like
Poles never cease to repulse. With new selves
Made when magnets are cut, as with old, aches

Will be cured, if you rub lodestone on skin.
Adulterers are unmasked if the pointer
Of a compass turns from them. Repulsion
'Deformates' worlds. *La vita activa*

Drives spiritual force through all human souls:
Proves eternal life; iron's worth over gold's.

V.

Plants and Animals

In the art of grafting to make a new plant
The alien material must be
Aligned to the structure, like magnets' want
To be aligned through God's necessity.

Living tissue harbours iron; magnetite
Crystals rest quietly inside trout, bees.
The bar-tailed godwit which flies through the night
Across the earth carries protein which *sees*,

Tracing invisible, circulating
Fields. The same is true for turtles, pigeons.
Friend of Drake, Hakluyt – for Gilbert, shipping
Was means to expand the rule of nations:

Since his terrellas can measure needle-dips,
Now Earth's Poles can show latitude on ships.

VI.

Music

Mahomet's coffin hovered, suspended
In mid-air by an arch of thick lodestones –
The pilgrims to Mecha stood, stupended
To explain the seer's miraculous bones.

Just so our wonder at musical notes,
Their attraction or repulsion, tonal
Or atonal, as their magnetic power floats
Between one chord and another chord's pull.

Tensions are set up, meanings will resound,
Harsh French *adamants* elide to *aimants*.
Shock might be instilled by an uncouth sound,
Harmony regained through strange alliance.

And one day the Poles might suddenly switch,
South change to North, their resonance drain from each.

Sudden Deafness

Spring days, Ardleigh woods were full of voices:
pigeons cooed in the tops of oaks, thrushes
and blackbirds shrilled in the grey-blue distance.
A lake wash of bluebells shone round the trunks.
Patter of yellow chicks, in the small runs
he had set up, brown pheasant hens clucking
over their shivering brood. He heard late winter
wind stir across the woods' floor, carefully
lifted the crying, ungainly birds back
into the hutches, settling chicks in straw.
By Autumn, the raucous, grown, clutch would screech
from the brakes, scurrying from beaters and guns.
But, since that morning when he woke stone deaf,
and they evicted him onto the dole,
what he most missed were Spring's sounds, woodland noise,
as he wandered roads, lost in strange silence.

Intimations

The lump on your leg was growing, hardening,
it had swollen beyond the explicable.
In the waiting room for the scan, we rehearsed
what it might be, but surely was not,
scared from knowing what it might come to mean.
When you were called, moments of awkwardness,
clumsy hugs as you went in, halted smiles
in front of the nurse. Only quickly
for you to reappear, struggling with rings,
with the fiddly clasps of your thin necklaces,
none of them allowed in the machine. I waited,
my taut fingers and wrists oddly bedecked;
the chains and too-small rings suspended
in blank air, losing your warmth, not gaining mine.

Lawrence's Craft

He had failed again; he could not retrieve
his drunk father from the *Three Tuns*, where he'd been
sent to fetch him. Tall stories of male deeds
at the pit were thronging the smoky air.
Sent packing, he shrugged dejected back home.

His hands blackened when he took the thin chisel
to the brick of coal, working to shape it
after its blank millennia deep in earth,
then to incise a deeper groove through the centre,
a runnel to hold his pens through its dark core.

Gestures of Grace

(for Sam)

Dürer-hands, a sunning butterfly
opening and closing its wings' bright dust for us,
then away:
I want my reading book.

Reaching upward, both hands fledgling beaks
silently flexing for food; coral mouths sifting
sea for spoil:
Tired; I need carrying.

A swift screw-movement above a bottle,
circling of forefinger before shower-tap
or door-knob:
Please open this for me.

And, at Allan Bank, before the vast
window looking over the lake, the mountains,
palms raised up:
See what I can show you.

Behind the Clock

The furniture's bulk loomed
over him where he crouched
before her dressing table.
The dancer pirouetted on her steel pin,
pink tutu tripled in the minute
mirrors of the music box,
its flip-up brass key tight
to turn for his young boy's fingers.
Only a few bars of the waltz
plinked out each time
after those cold fingers tired; but still
he thrilled as, plastic arm
gracefully raised, scarlet lips
catching the tiny mirrors' light,
round she spun till the mechanism
wound down again.

Was it he, shivering in school shorts,
wondering at the miraculous
dancer, who was the ghost in
this sphere; or they, adult voices
shimmering sporadically
from the room below
through the ceiling of their underworld?
For they threatened again and again
that his sins and misbehaviour
would send him to that other realm,
open some small door in Nanny's room
behind the clock, draw him in,
then hold him on the other side of a wall
through which he would never break
through to where they were again.

Stilled Lives

Not the bodies,
                but
the silence round
      the bodies,
the red clay
         particling the air

lava-mote aura
       defining
what it caught
      in its moment's shaping

petrified mother grappling her child,
man cowering his head
           down

against the radiating
         ash-storm

In the Eye of the Horse

With both sons, the wind brunted
the struggle across trammelled

ground to the burial-place,
to that ditch-ringed hillside,

stronghold against untold threats;
and then our fearful slide, down

through limned skull-curvature
to the iris-less eye.

We clawed at earth with chill
knuckle-bones, pushed the navel-cords

into the hard soil, scant overlay.
Who knows what else of you both

we left out there beyond
our selves, to be unsettled

by winter storms, or soothed
in the livelong hold of fragile skies?

Looking at Late Rembrandts

(after leaving Dad at the Nursing Home)

Bodies strained upright
in upright
straight-backed chairs;
struggle to stay
still,
      clawing hands
grappling arm-rests to brace;
their skin-shrunk
           rounded
skulls
      concentrated
by some inexpressive
thought,

the life that has lived them,

the eyes stunned
by seeing the what
is not there,
the foreseeable
that has happened
          to them;
the eyes in the
struck faces
of the painter's sitters
alone

alive
with a lead-white

glint of light.

Last Christmas Cracker

From the last Christmas cracker I pulled ever
with Dad, it seemed there flew not just the golf-tees
I will never use, but my yellow kite
the line broke from, and the wind wafted
into the tall oak where he climbed to get it;
my blue wooden yacht which grounded itself
in the middle of the council boating lake,
where he waded barefoot through the sludge
to restore it sodden to the concrete shore;
the garage window I broke one Sunday
learning to curve a shot round the linen post;
then, in a terrible rush, all the things
in the future he will not ever set
to rights, now that he has gone away.

Tanto…Tanto

'It's because I've lived so much
that I want to live so much more'
(Pablo Neruda)

Olive-tree slopes, orange
soil shelving to azure
middle-sea, the morning
awaiting the sun's blaze.

It's some blinding Spanish
country of the mind
(so much, and too much):
so much the bask of light

as the cloud-blear lifts
from the slopes of El Cielo;
and as the sun frees, upon
the bodice-fans of thick leaves,

cicadas to their buzz-squall
of chatter, to fandangos
that survive the habits
of inevitable song.

The Crystallographer

(Dorothy Hodgkin)

I.

Tessera by tessera,
centuries of Egyptian
sand are eased away.

Patterns of reds, blues,
greens break through
the grains as the brush

strokes across them,
and the mosaic is
gradually unearthed.

A teenager, she crouches
for days shielded
from the sun's blare,

her one-tenth
to scale drawings
emerging into life

as she adds colour
to reveal the tesserae's
repeating pattern.

II.

Intuitively,
her feet find the rungs
of the wooden ladder,

raised and let down, hand-cranked
on taut wires through pulleys.
Thick double-bayed window-

arches and bricked vaulting
hold out nighttime,
hold in silence.

She lowers herself
and her tray
of glass fibres

and shellacked crystals.
She mounts
each minute strand

in the goniometer,
switches up
the unearthed

AC current
drilled through
the lab's two metre

thick wall, then
draws and photos
the x-ray

refractions through
her dyed crystals.
The lattice-work

of atoms flowers
on the photographic plates.
The repeating structure

clarifies for her, except
where birefringence
conjures momently

ghost-spots,
a confusion between
the waves' peaks and troughs,

like the mirages
which shimmered
in sands near Khartoum.

The Earth Turned Upside Down

At dawn, crazed contrails
in the snow, some errant god
trampling the white heavens
in vengeance:

or Phaeton's chariot-marks, maybe,
once his freaked horse-team
has gone out of control,
the wheels slewing
all over,

with time itself become confused,
the dark of day, light of night,

through all of which careers
the pursuing Jove,
frantic to enforce order.

The Hand

held beneath
my hand as we try
to raise the beaker
to dry, peeled lips
is blackberry-stained
by eczema,
as we both
work to bring
the plastic teat
to be clenched between
gums, to tilt it
in spite of the shaking
of that hand and the head,
so that cranberry
might for more moments
ease the prostate pain;
the hand held beneath
my hand that once cradled
my baby hand, teaching
me once and for all
to drink

Stanzas

Venice, the waters' vocalise
a worked meander
along the canals
churned by
vaporettos between
gondolas between
funeral barges lurched along
weed-decked palace walls.

Sealight at-a-dapple,
sunlight solid
in piazzas empty
of their own music,
chambers for wordless song
resounding with the waters.

Snapshots

I.

Roped to a tree,
drenched purple and yellow petals
against stripped-pale bark,
memorial flowers in foil
outside Ruskin's cathedral
to the steady creeping
progress of life

II.

Intimacy awakens us
as you rest, clenched
in the shrouding duvet,
larva coiled upon itself
about to writhe around
on to its back and shrug off
another of its skins

III.

The lanterns, moons,
the shadows, humans
striding the treetops;
the moveless waters
indifferent, singed
by swift sparks, the dipping
fireflies

IV.

Us as summer afternoon lovers
behind bloomed-into glass,
shielded by thin curtains
and the more bared by the heat;
attentive to the day's exchanges nearby,
children's high hilarity
on the swings in playground sunlight

Gut, Not Steel

Take a plectrum
        to the sky

and prick out
        lyre-songs

that wring
        from the cloudedness
        the tears
        it is so earnest

with concealing

Twinkle, Twinkle

The wall-chart's stars were yellow dots, white lines
linking them into named constellations;

Orion with his belt and sword-holder,
the tilted dubelyoo of Cassiopeia.

He lay admiring their gleam, stars and moon
passing thin curtains in his teenage bedroom.

(Such memories recur to re-tune me,
wherever I've lived far from that first home.)

Yet he knew, when Cordelia salves fever
that set jangling the mind of her father,

casting Lear to roam the heath, soft music,
then louder, is conjured to work physic;

yet neither she nor he doubts luckless stars
will part them, guided by discordant fears.

Sketches for Composition

(Mahler, Symphony no. 3 in D Minor)

I.

Harm is from the air.

Now, it is *Chalara fraxinea*
arrives on the winds,
ash-trees crackling,
limbs desiccated from the core out.

One foundered trunk,
its branches stunted arms,
its knoll an anguished head,
is a pietà in rutted mud.

Leaf-cover has become slow
rain into its own forest,
now stark and naked
beneath the ever-lowering skies.

II.

In this hazed light, it is hard to see across
to the river's other bank. The grey shapes
loomed there, pixelated by the dark-falling,
have our height, are uncomfortable in stance,
their stooping shoulders so familiar.

Leaves silhouette the blue-black sky; the sun,
blank disc on the matte behind them, makes
a quick-silver mirror of the river-light –
of them, a negative print of us –
the livid cold thread of the river still between.

Our selves, quieting, have not yet found their stay,
we wandering and returning to the brink;
if we did jostle amongst them, theirs would be
the flinch of the dead at the reek of the living.

But please,
do not let this be the slow lightening of dawn,
the palette shifting black to inky blue.

III.

Is the movement to; beyond desire
the returned-to; place which might move
(vertigo in tightening embrace)

rare full naked looking of eyes
into eyes,
rare softening of a face under

caress;
the quiet once-hard breathing
reciprocally stills, hearts' rise

*

Your bare back turned to me takes all my breath;
Your muscles' complex sheen is wind's stealth
Across a field of wheat.
Glimpsed through the doorway, for you to give the wealth
Of yourself, to turn and bring quickened faith
To my heart with the heat
In your loving eyes, would kill those monsters
You otherwise adore, forge our shared desires.

*

I try to synchronize
my breath with yours, thinking
to calm us tired both in-
to sleep, establish rhy-
thm, hope to break frets
stammering the day long;
everything slows, flows, ebbs,
your cheek weighs heavier
against my heart until
the room is lost to itself. Only
then you suddenly shift
away, my heart flinching
colder, and we snap back
into at-odds awakeness

IV.
Human ashes take long to sift
through sieve-holes
of a dented brass censer
swung over a sodden municipal lawn.

The council worker,
sweating January rain
in his too-large stage black,
stumbles *In the midst of life*
from a torn photocopy,
as still your ashes stream
from his sugar-shaker.

There are no bees to pollinate
the flowers in the fields
after the turn towards Spring.
Drenched cellulose
in stem walls reaches
the heads vertical, petals
ablaze, pistils untouched
in finite, silenced, air.

V.

That the
pebble-shaped shells of others –
dream-pure cerulean or
                                speckled by hopes
and fears – are readily splayed
                                on the earth.

That the
lone note in still, winter-time woods –
light clenching to dark over fresh-ploughed fields –
harbingers nothing
        as the floods renew.

That the
cleansing from homes and land –
bulldozers wrenching roofs, collapsing walls –
            sees humans as
learning nothing from birds, their new-built
nests that will proliferate next Spring.

VI.

That heaven resides in flowers' opening
That flowers are soft-tender to hands' tearing
That cats are to be met by feet dancing

That fingers flexed in air are fascinating
That a grown-up's big voice is terror-making
That that tentative first-ever smile is devastating

That the present is the place of meaning

But that

the dead do abide.

They seem, in wall cavities,
in what we breathe.

If you're coming to bed come now.

At extreme moments, we are
beside.
Open me. I have a

void to show you.

It is nice to feel you inside me again.

Last Song

(Joseph von Eichendorff)

In our up-times, in our feuds,
We've wandered hand in hand;
Now we come to our resting-place,
After drifting the still land.

All round, valleys plunge to the depths,
The sky is blackening;
Two larks alone rise,
In our balmy night-dreaming.

Leave them to fly, and touch me;
Soon, we'll flag from weariness,
Fearful we'll be left astray
In our solitariness.

The endless silent fret
Deepens towards sunset.
For us, worn from the constant onset,
Is this darkness dawning death?

Notes

'Airs'

John Wilbye is the leading English madrigal composer. He lived in retirement in Colchester and died there in 1638. The madrigals for which these new words were written are

I. *My throat is sore, my voice is hoarse with skriking*;
II. *When shall my wretched life give place to death?*;
III. *Ye that do live in pleasures plenty.*

Wilbye was commemorated in a small case of relics in the Colchester Castle Museum, alongside other local worthies, William Gilbert, 'the magnetism man', and Ann and Jane Taylor, who wrote the nursery rhyme 'Twinkle, Twinkle, Little Star'. I was fascinated as a child by this particular glass cabinet on our various school and family trips to the Museum.

New words to Wilbye's *Fly not so swift, my dear, behold me dying* appear as the central section of 'Sketches for Composition' III.

'William Gilbert: *On Magnetism*'

Gilbert was the Court Physician to Elizabeth I from 1601 to her death in 1603. But he retained close ties to the town of his birth, Colchester, across his life. He is buried in Holy Trinity Church, just across the road from his home there, Tymperley's. Gilbert's house survives today, in an inner town courtyard amidst much red shopping-centre brickwork. Gilbert's New Latin text, *De Magnete*, was published in 1600, and coined the word 'electricus' ('like amber'), a word soon translated as 'electricity'. Gilbert was the first scientist who identified the centre of the Earth as iron; his experiments moving needles across the surface of what he called 'terrellas', spheres cut from lodestone, enabled advances in navigation. Gilbert was also the first person to realise that magnets might be cut into sections, with each section forming a new magnet, its Poles intact. Sonnet VI, 'Music', adapts ideas spoken in interview by the contemporary composer, Thomas Adès, as reported in *The Guardian*, 12.9.12.

'Sketches for Composition'

As Gustav Mahler sketched his Third Symphony in 1895, he developed
a putative set of titles for the six movements. The poems in my sequence
respond both to the music of the final work, and to the titles which
Mahler originally listed:

I. What the forest tells me;
II. What the twilight tells me;
III. What love tells me;
IV. What the flowers of the field tell me;
V. What the cuckoo tells me;
VI. What the child tells me.

In other versions of the programme, Mahler called the last movement
'What God tells me'.

The von Eichendorff poem imitated in 'Last Song' is 'Im Abendrot'
('At Twilight'); it was set as the last of Richard Strauss's *Vier Letze Lieder*
('Four Last Songs') (1947–8).

Two Rivers Press has been publishing in and about Reading since 1994. Founded by the artist Peter Hay (1951–2003), the press continues to delight readers, local and further afield, with its varied list of individually designed, thought-provoking books.